90°

120°   60°

150°   30°

180°   0°

210°   330°

240°   300°

270°

$\frac{7\pi}{12}$ $\frac{\pi}{2}$ $\frac{5\pi}{12}$

$\frac{2\pi}{3}$ $\frac{\pi}{3}$

$\frac{3\pi}{4}$ $\frac{\pi}{4}$

$\frac{5\pi}{6}$ $\frac{\pi}{6}$

$\frac{11\pi}{12}$ $\frac{\pi}{12}$

π 0

$\frac{13\pi}{12}$ $\frac{23\pi}{12}$

$\frac{7\pi}{6}$ $\frac{11\pi}{6}$

$\frac{5\pi}{4}$ $\frac{7\pi}{4}$

$\frac{4\pi}{3}$ $\frac{5\pi}{3}$

$\frac{17\pi}{12}$ $\frac{3\pi}{2}$ $\frac{19\pi}{12}$

1													
2													
3													
4													
5													
6													
7													
8													
9													
10													
11													
12													
13													
14													
15													
16													
17													
18													
19													
20													
21													
22													
23													
24													
25													
26													
27													
28													
29													
30													
31													
32													
33													
34													
35													
36													
37													
38													

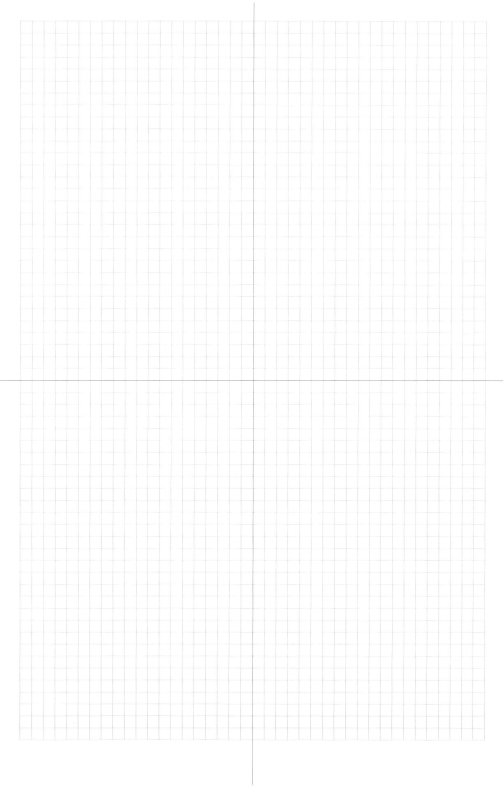

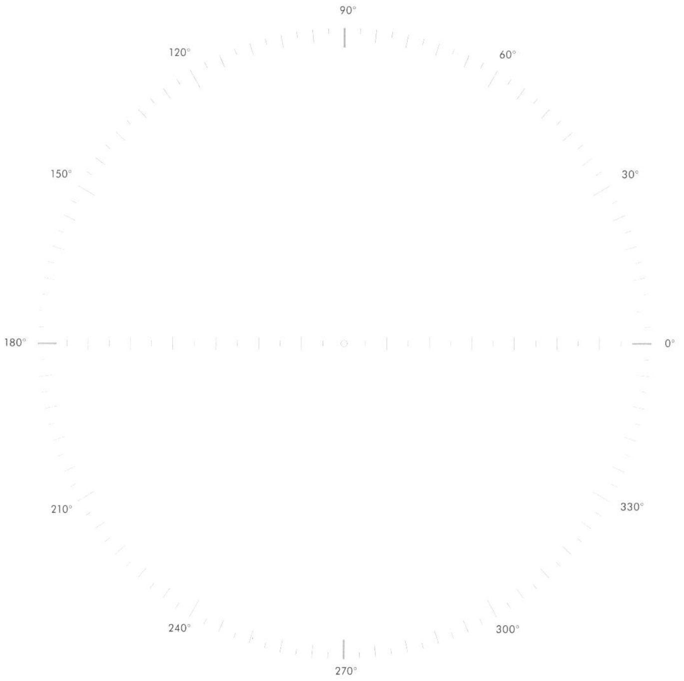

90°

120°   60°

150°   30°

180° —————   ————— 0°

210°   330°

240°   300°

270°

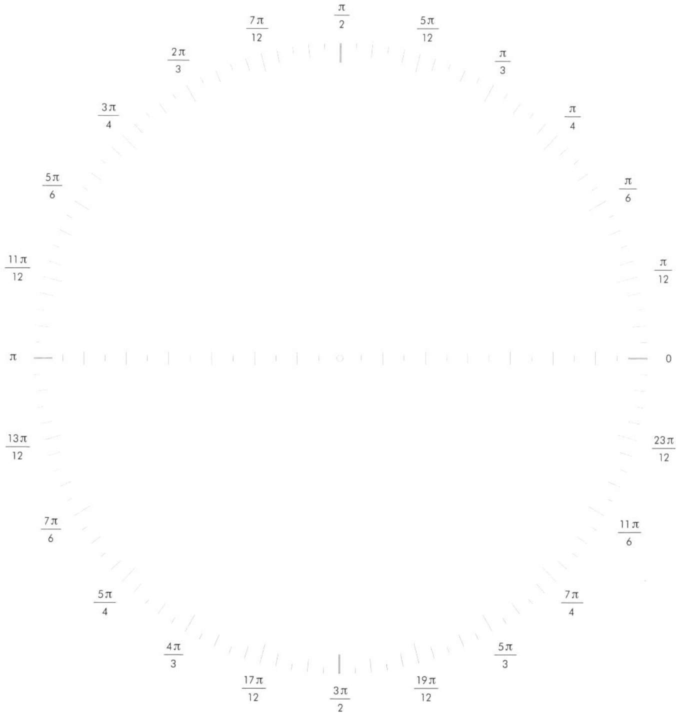

$\frac{7\pi}{12}$ $\frac{\pi}{2}$ $\frac{5\pi}{12}$

$\frac{2\pi}{3}$ $\frac{\pi}{3}$

$\frac{3\pi}{4}$ $\frac{\pi}{4}$

$\frac{5\pi}{6}$ $\frac{\pi}{6}$

$\frac{11\pi}{12}$ $\frac{\pi}{12}$

π —————   ————— 0

$\frac{13\pi}{12}$ $\frac{23\pi}{12}$

$\frac{7\pi}{6}$ $\frac{11\pi}{6}$

$\frac{5\pi}{4}$ $\frac{7\pi}{4}$

$\frac{4\pi}{3}$ $\frac{5\pi}{3}$

$\frac{17\pi}{12}$ $\frac{3\pi}{2}$ $\frac{19\pi}{12}$

1													
2													
3													
4													
5													
6													
7													
8													
9													
10													
11													
12													
13													
14													
15													
16													
17													
18													
19													
20													
21													
22													
23													
24													
25													
26													
27													
28													
29													
30													
31													
32													
33													
34													
35													
36													
37													
38													

GEOMETRY

SQUARE

$A = a^2$

$P = 4a$

RECTANGLE

$A = ab$

$P = 2a + 2b$

TRAPEZOID

$A = h\dfrac{a+b}{2}$

$P = a + b + c + d$

PARALLELOGRAM

$A = bh$

$P = 2a + 2b$

RHOMBUS

$A = \dfrac{1}{2} d_1 d_2$

TRIANGLE

$A = \dfrac{1}{2} bh$

$P = a + b + c$

RIGHT TRIANGLE
(PYTHAGOREAN THEOREM)

$a^2 + b^2 = c^2$

CIRCLE

$A = \pi r^2$

$P = 2\pi r$

RECTANGULAR PRISM

$V = abc$

$S = 2ab + 2ac + 2bc$

CONE

$V = \dfrac{1}{3} \pi r^2 h$

$S = \pi r^2 + \pi r a$

CYLINDER

$V = \pi r^2 h$

$S = 2\pi r(r + h)$

SPHERE

$V = \dfrac{4}{3} \pi r^3$

$S = 4\pi r^2$

GOLDEN RATIO

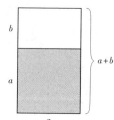

$$\dfrac{a+b}{a} = \dfrac{a}{b} = \phi = 1.6180339887...$$

EULER'S POLYHEDRON THEOREM

The number of faces (f), vertices (v), and edges (e) of a convex polyhedron are related by the formula:

$f + v = e + 2$

Rhombic Dodecahedron

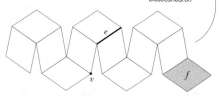

For the twelve basic shapes shown above, equations are given for area (A), perimeter (P), volume (V) and surface area (S).

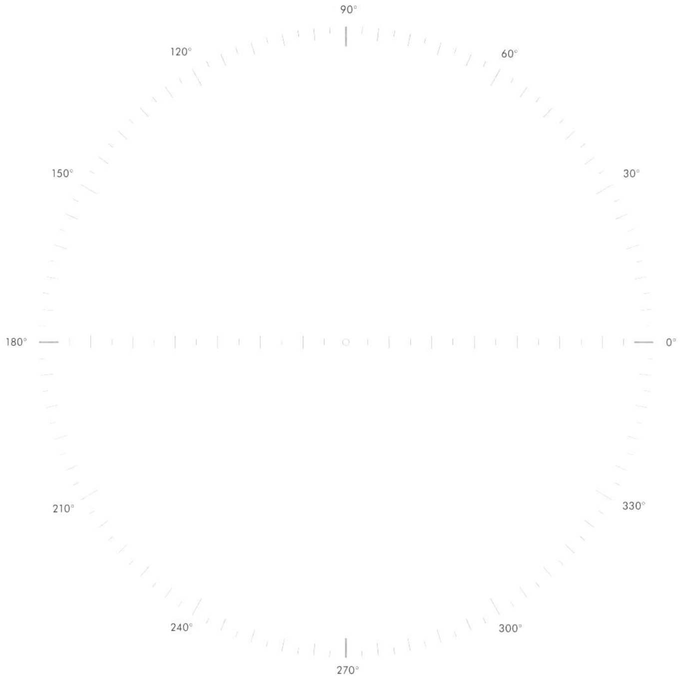

90°

120°   60°

150°   30°

180° — ○ — 0°

210°   330°

240°   300°

270°

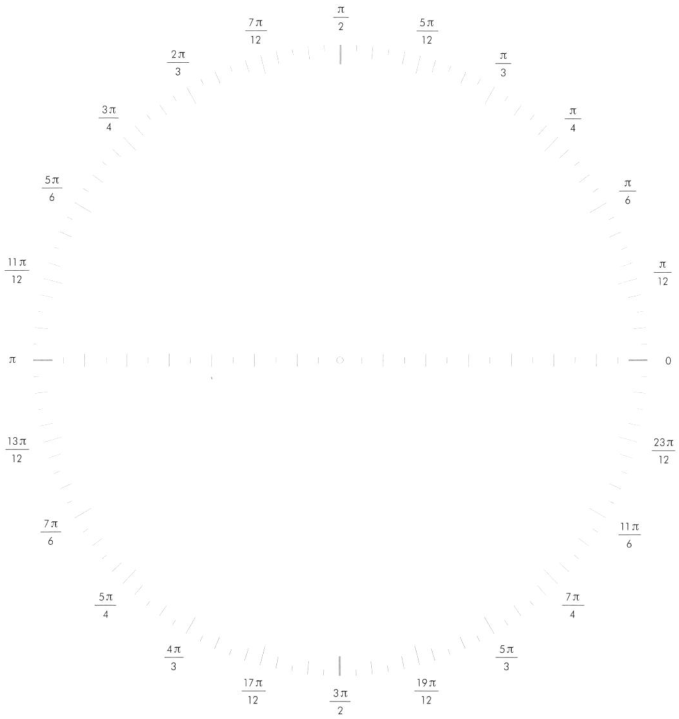

$\frac{\pi}{2}$

$\frac{7\pi}{12}$ $\frac{5\pi}{12}$

$\frac{2\pi}{3}$ $\frac{\pi}{3}$

$\frac{3\pi}{4}$ $\frac{\pi}{4}$

$\frac{5\pi}{6}$ $\frac{\pi}{6}$

$\frac{11\pi}{12}$ $\frac{\pi}{12}$

π — ○ — 0

$\frac{13\pi}{12}$ $\frac{23\pi}{12}$

$\frac{7\pi}{6}$ $\frac{11\pi}{6}$

$\frac{5\pi}{4}$ $\frac{7\pi}{4}$

$\frac{4\pi}{3}$ $\frac{5\pi}{3}$

$\frac{17\pi}{12}$ $\frac{3\pi}{2}$ $\frac{19\pi}{12}$

1									
2									
3									
4									
5									
6									
7									
8									
9									
10									
11									
12									
13									
14									
15									
16									
17									
18									
19									
20									
21									
22									
23									
24									
25									
26									
27									
28									
29									
30									
31									
32									
33									
34									
35									
36									
37									
38									

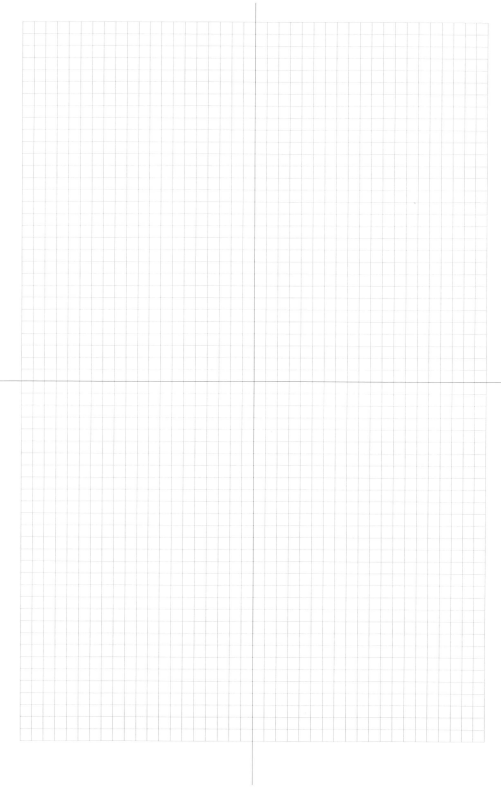

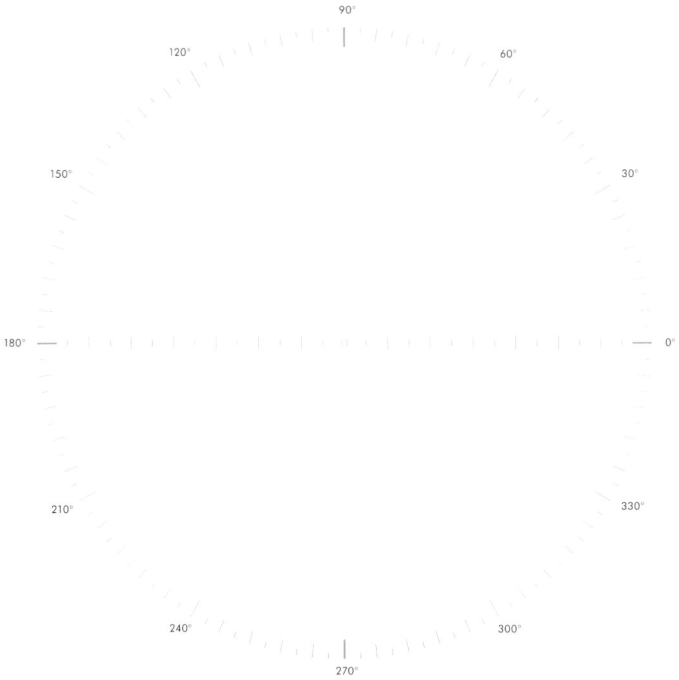

90°

120°   60°

150°   30°

180°   0°

210°   330°

240°   300°

270°

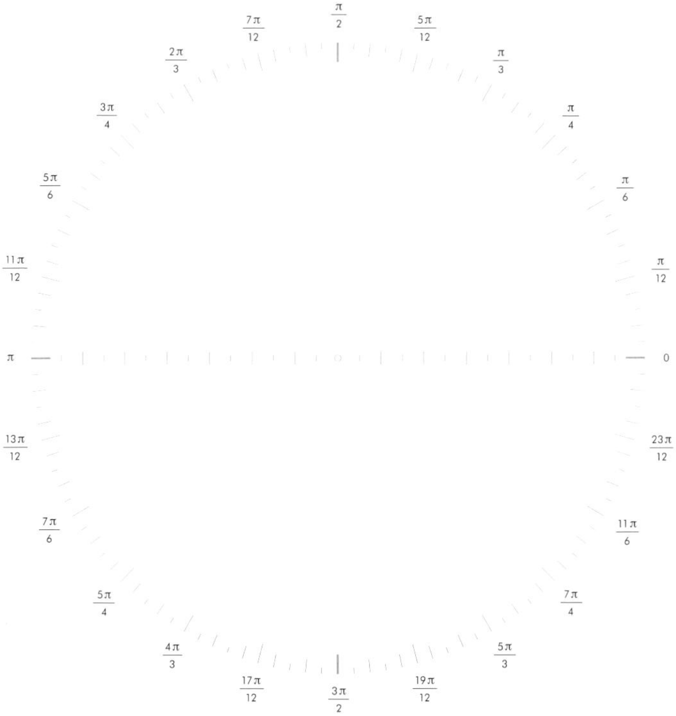

$\frac{\pi}{2}$

$\frac{7\pi}{12}$ $\frac{5\pi}{12}$

$\frac{2\pi}{3}$ $\frac{\pi}{3}$

$\frac{3\pi}{4}$ $\frac{\pi}{4}$

$\frac{5\pi}{6}$ $\frac{\pi}{6}$

$\frac{11\pi}{12}$ $\frac{\pi}{12}$

π 0

$\frac{13\pi}{12}$ $\frac{23\pi}{12}$

$\frac{7\pi}{6}$ $\frac{11\pi}{6}$

$\frac{5\pi}{4}$ $\frac{7\pi}{4}$

$\frac{4\pi}{3}$ $\frac{5\pi}{3}$

$\frac{17\pi}{12}$ $\frac{3\pi}{2}$ $\frac{19\pi}{12}$

1												
2												
3												
4												
5												
6												
7												
8												
9												
10												
11												
12												
13												
14												
15												
16												
17												
18												
19												
20												
21												
22												
23												
24												
25												
26												
27												
28												
29												
30												
31												
32												
33												
34												
35												
36												
37												
38												

ALTERNATIVE ALPHABETS

	PHONETIC	BRAILLE	SEMAPHORE	ASL	MORSE CODE		PHONETIC	BRAILLE	SEMAPHORE	ASL	MORSE CODE
A	alpha					S	sierra				
B	bravo					T	tango				
C	charlie					U	uniform				
D	delta					V	victor				
E	echo					W	whiskey				
F	foxtrot					X	x-ray				
G	golf					Y	yankee				
H	hotel					Z	zulu				
I	india					1	one				
J	juliet					2	two				
K	kilo					3	three				
L	lima					4	four				
M	mike					5	five				
N	november					6	six				
O	oscar					7	seven				
P	papa					8	eight				
Q	quebec					9	nine				
R	romeo					0	zero				

With braille and semaphore, the first ten letters also represent numerals. Use and as numeral prefixes.

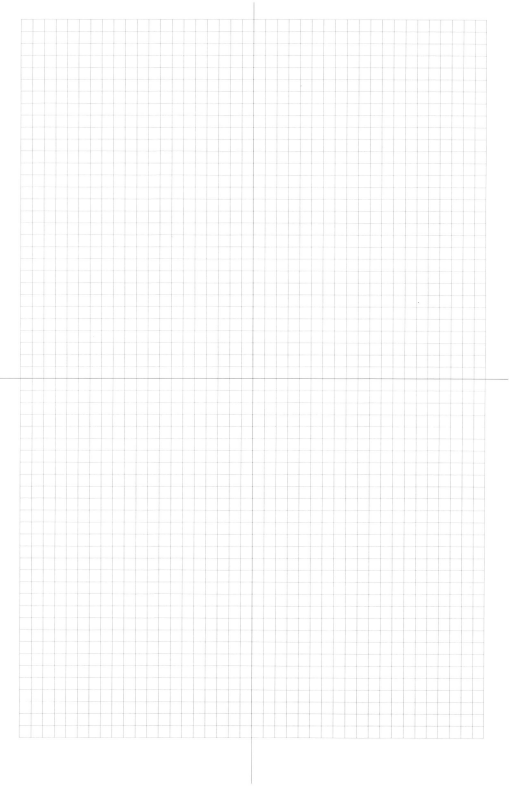

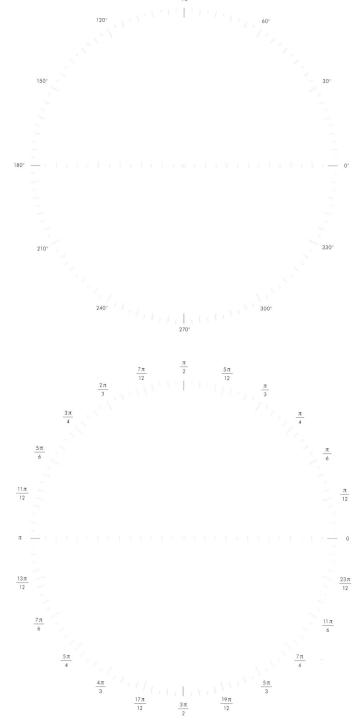

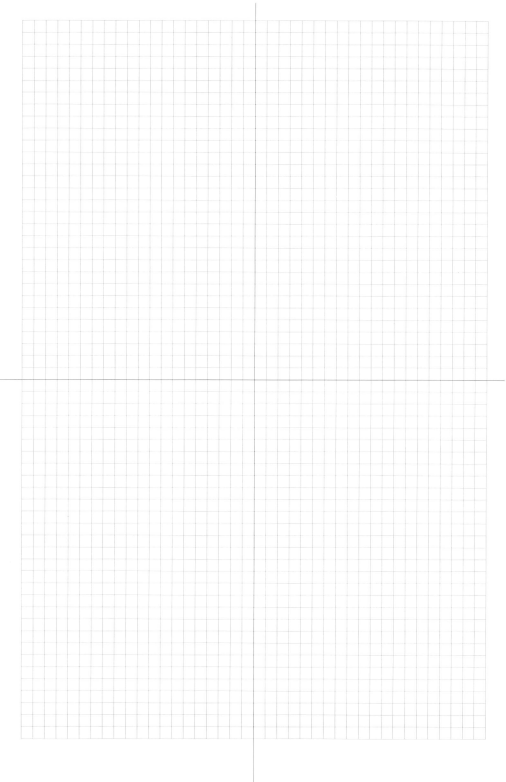

90°

120°   60°

150°   30°

180°   0°

210°   330°

240°   300°

270°

$\frac{7\pi}{12}$ $\frac{\pi}{2}$ $\frac{5\pi}{12}$

$\frac{2\pi}{3}$ $\frac{\pi}{3}$

$\frac{3\pi}{4}$ $\frac{\pi}{4}$

$\frac{5\pi}{6}$ $\frac{\pi}{6}$

$\frac{11\pi}{12}$ $\frac{\pi}{12}$

π 0

$\frac{13\pi}{12}$ $\frac{23\pi}{12}$

$\frac{7\pi}{6}$ $\frac{11\pi}{6}$

$\frac{5\pi}{4}$ $\frac{7\pi}{4}$

$\frac{4\pi}{3}$ $\frac{5\pi}{3}$

$\frac{17\pi}{12}$ $\frac{3\pi}{2}$ $\frac{19\pi}{12}$

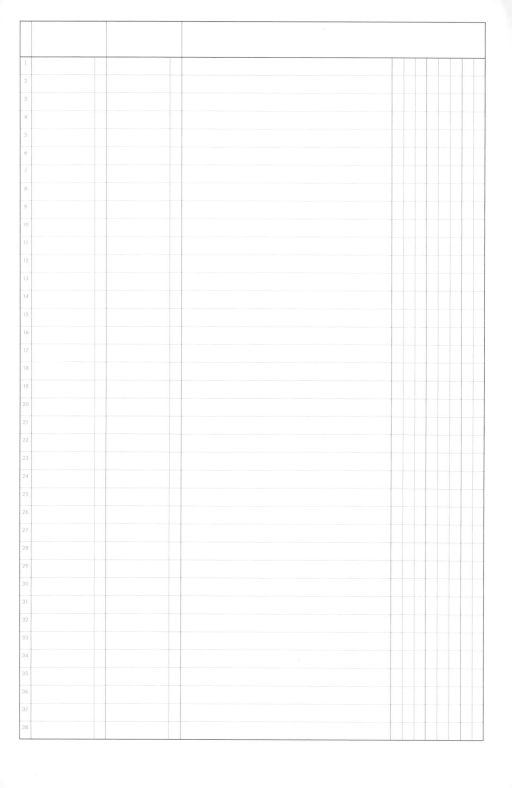

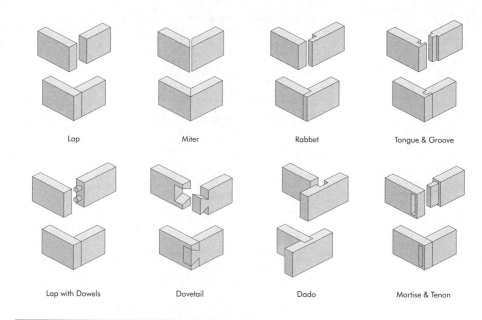

| Lap | Miter | Rabbet | Tongue & Groove |

| Lap with Dowels | Dovetail | Dado | Mortise & Tenon |

Gauge	Max. head diameter (in.)	SHANK DIAMETER		ROOT DIAMETER		Threads per inch
		Basic decimal size (in.)	Nearest fractional equivalent	Average decimal size (in.)	Nearest fractional equivalent	
0	.119	.060	1/16	.040	3/64	32
1	.146	.073	5/64	.046	3/64	28
2	.172	.086	3/32	.054	1/16	26
3	.199	.099	7/64	.065	1/16	24
4	.225	.112	7/64	.075	5/64	22
5	.252	.125	1/8	.085	5/64	20
6	.279	.138	9/64	.094	3/32	18
7	.305	.151	5/32	.102	7/64	16
8	.332	.164	5/32	.112	7/64	15
9	.358	.177	11/64	.122	1/8	14
10	.385	.190	3/16	.130	1/8	13
11	.411	.203	13/64	.139	9/64	12
12	.438	.216	7/32	.148	9/64	11
14	.491	.242	1/4	.165	5/32	10
16	.544	.268	17/64	.184	3/16	9
18	.597	.294	19/64	.204	13/64	8
20	.650	.320	5/16	.233	7/32	8
24	.756	.372	3/8	.260	1/4	7

COUNTERSUNK

OVAL

ROUND

Length

Shank diameter

Root diameter

PAN

TRUSS

BUTTON/DOME

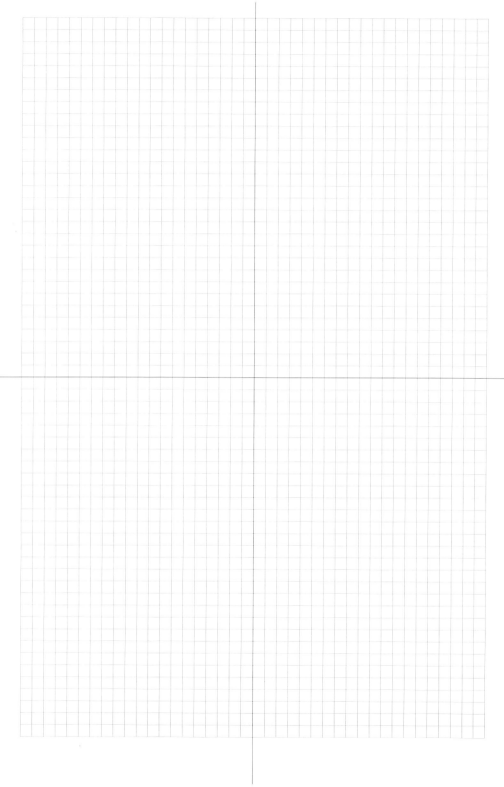

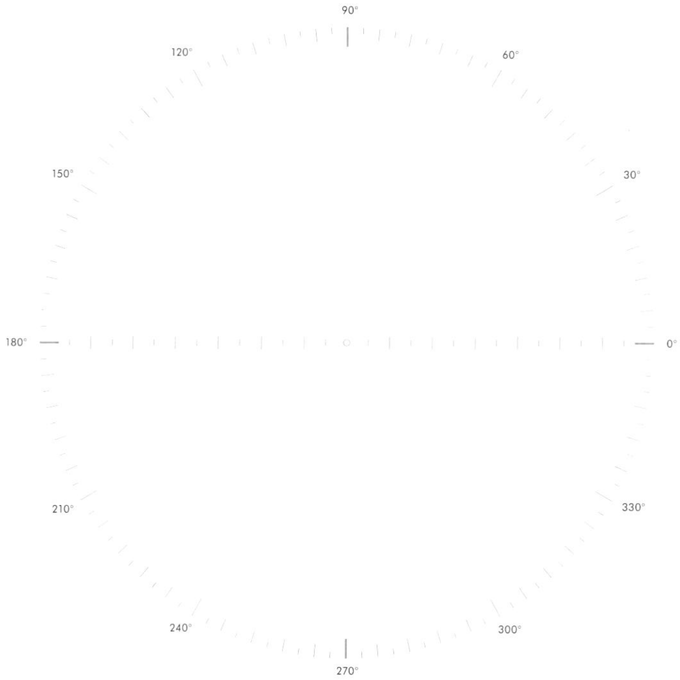

$90°$

$120°$ $60°$

$150°$ $30°$

$180°$ $0°$

$210°$ $330°$

$240°$ $300°$

$270°$

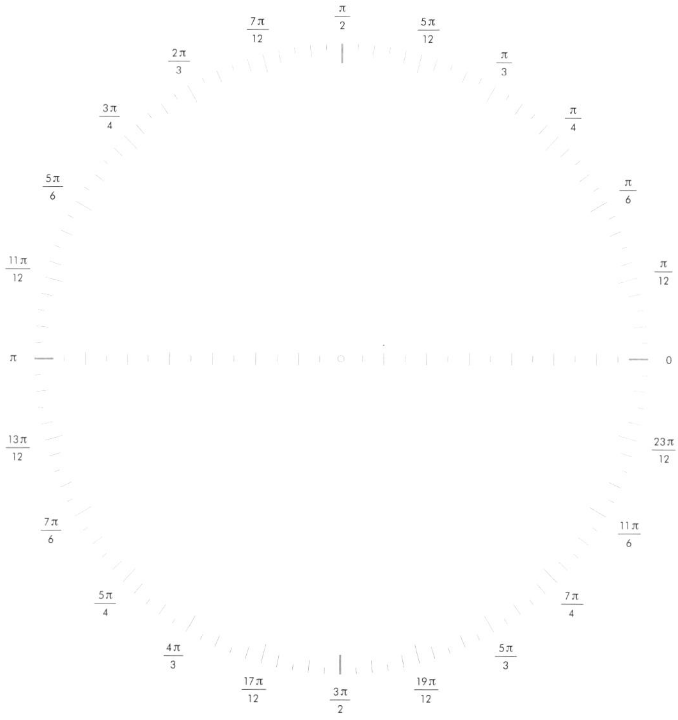

$\dfrac{7\pi}{12}$ $\dfrac{\pi}{2}$ $\dfrac{5\pi}{12}$

$\dfrac{2\pi}{3}$ $\dfrac{\pi}{3}$

$\dfrac{3\pi}{4}$ $\dfrac{\pi}{4}$

$\dfrac{5\pi}{6}$ $\dfrac{\pi}{6}$

$\dfrac{11\pi}{12}$ $\dfrac{\pi}{12}$

π 0

$\dfrac{13\pi}{12}$ $\dfrac{23\pi}{12}$

$\dfrac{7\pi}{6}$ $\dfrac{11\pi}{6}$

$\dfrac{5\pi}{4}$ $\dfrac{7\pi}{4}$

$\dfrac{4\pi}{3}$ $\dfrac{5\pi}{3}$

$\dfrac{17\pi}{12}$ $\dfrac{3\pi}{2}$ $\dfrac{19\pi}{12}$

1												
2												
3												
4												
5												
6												
7												
8												
9												
10												
11												
12												
13												
14												
15												
16												
17												
18												
19												
20												
21												
22												
23												
24												
25												
26												
27												
28												
29												
30												
31												
32												
33												
34												
35												
36												
37												
38												

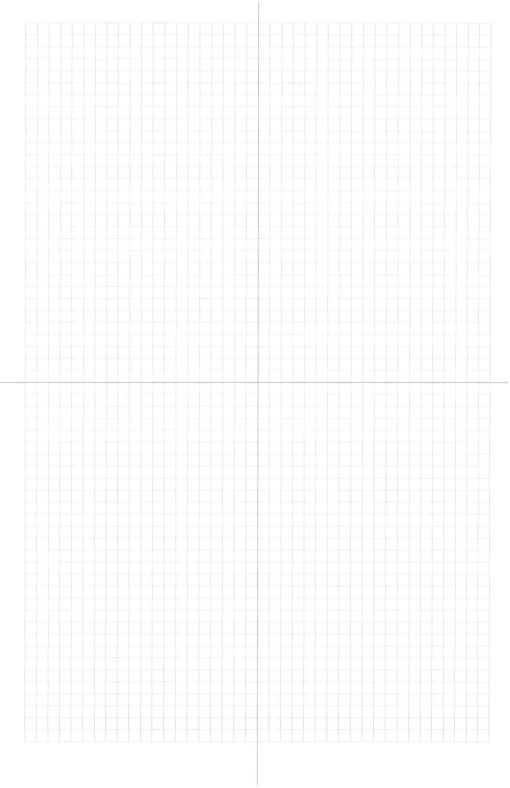

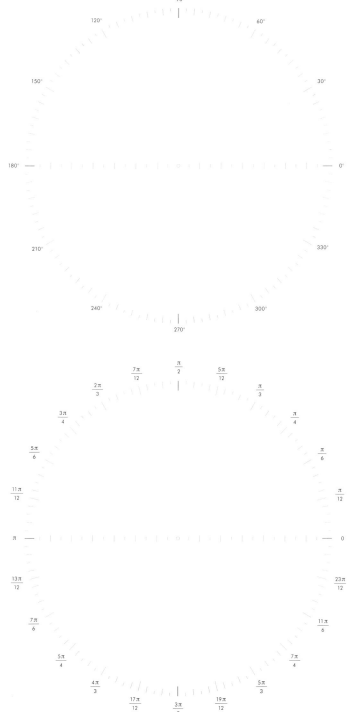

EARTH & THE SOLAR SYSTEM

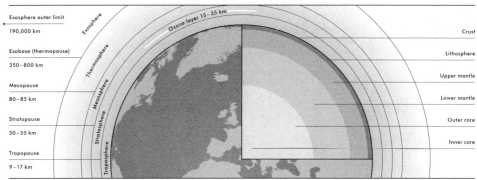

Exosphere outer limit
190,000 km

Exobase (thermopause)
350–800 km

Mesopause
80–85 km

Stratopause
50–55 km

Tropopause
9–17 km

Exosphere
Thermosphere
Mesosphere
Stratosphere
Troposphere

Ozone layer 15–35 km

Crust
Lithosphere
Upper mantle
Lower mantle
Outer core
Inner core

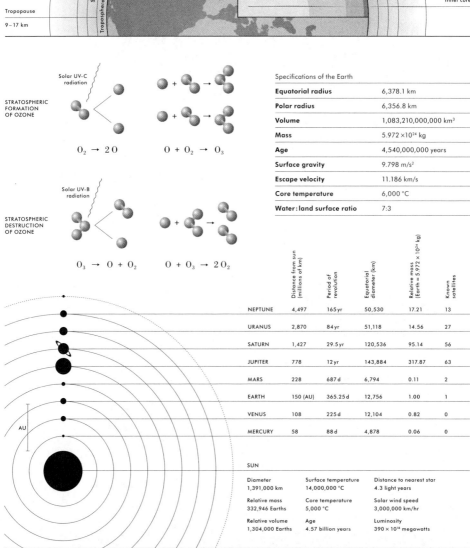

STRATOSPHERIC FORMATION OF OZONE

Solar UV-C radiation

$$O_2 \rightarrow 2\,O \qquad O + O_2 \rightarrow O_3$$

STRATOSPHERIC DESTRUCTION OF OZONE

Solar UV-B radiation

$$O_3 \rightarrow O + O_2 \qquad O + O_3 \rightarrow 2\,O_2$$

Specifications of the Earth

Equatorial radius	6,378.1 km
Polar radius	6,356.8 km
Volume	1,083,210,000,000 km³
Mass	5.972×10^{24} kg
Age	4,540,000,000 years
Surface gravity	9.798 m/s²
Escape velocity	11.186 km/s
Core temperature	6,000 °C
Water:land surface ratio	7:3

	Distance from sun (millions of km)	Period of revolution	Equatorial diameter (km)	Relative mass (Earth = 5.972×10^{24} kg)	Known satellites
NEPTUNE	4,497	165 yr	50,530	17.21	13
URANUS	2,870	84 yr	51,118	14.56	27
SATURN	1,427	29.5 yr	120,536	95.14	56
JUPITER	778	12 yr	143,884	317.87	63
MARS	228	687 d	6,794	0.11	2
EARTH	150 (AU)	365.25 d	12,756	1.00	1
VENUS	108	225 d	12,104	0.82	0
MERCURY	58	88 d	4,878	0.06	0

AU

SUN

Diameter 1,391,000 km	Surface temperature 14,000,000 °C	Distance to nearest star 4.3 light years
Relative mass 332,946 Earths	Core temperature 5,000 °C	Solar wind speed 3,000,000 km/hr
Relative volume 1,304,000 Earths	Age 4.57 billion years	Luminosity 390×10^{18} megawatts

An Astronomical Unit (AU) is the mean distance between the Earth and the Sun: 149,597,870,700 meters. *Distances and sizes are not drawn to scale.*

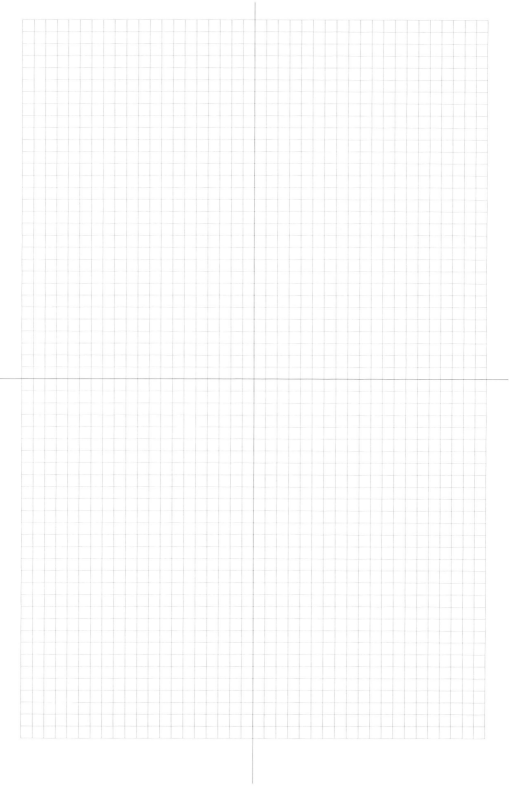

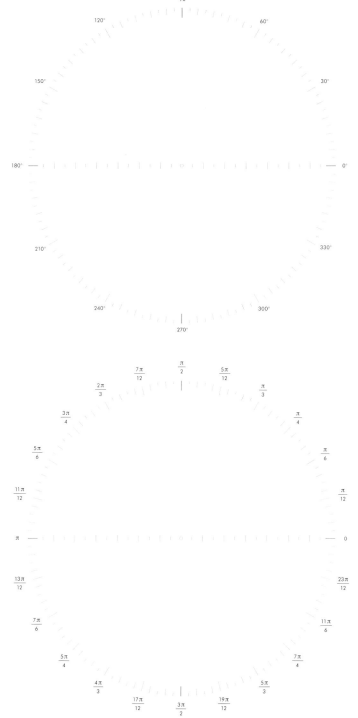

1												
2												
3												
4												
5												
6												
7												
8												
9												
10												
11												
12												
13												
14												
15												
16												
17												
18												
19												
20												
21												
22												
23												
24												
25												
26												
27												
28												
29												
30												
31												
32												
33												
34												
35												
36												
37												
38												

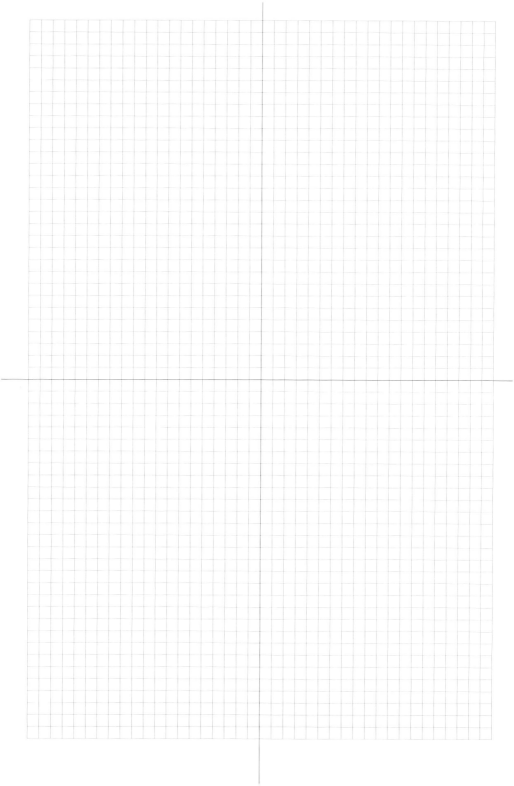

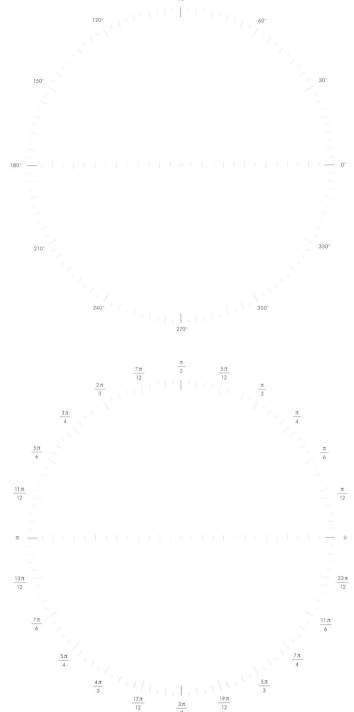

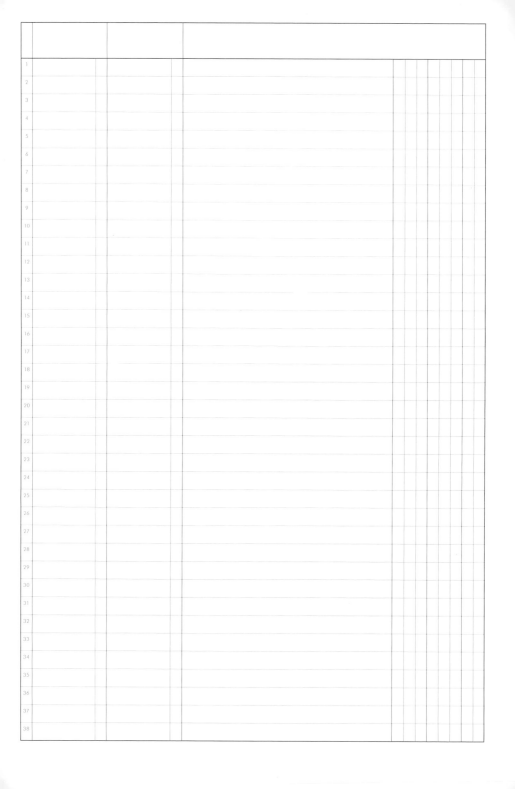

Key

group
element name
atomic number
Symbol
relative atomic mass

Legend

- Nonmetals
- Halogens
- Noble gases
- Metalloids
- Basic metals
- Transition metals
- (unknown properties)
- Inner transition metals
- Alkali metals
- Alkaline Earth metals

Period	1	2	3	4	5	6	7	8	9	10	11	12	13	14	15	16	17	18
1	hydrogen 1 **H** 1.0079																	helium 2 **He** 4.0026
2	lithium 3 **Li** 6.941	beryllium 4 **Be** 9.012											boron 5 **B** 10.811	carbon 6 **C** 12.011	nitrogen 7 **N** 14.007	oxygen 8 **O** 15.999	fluorine 9 **F** 18.998	neon 10 **Ne** 20.180
3	sodium 11 **Na** 22.990	magnesium 12 **Mg** 24.305											aluminum 13 **Al** 26.982	silicon 14 **Si** 28.086	phosphorus 15 **P** 30.974	sulfur 16 **S** 32.065	chlorine 17 **Cl** 35.453	argon 18 **Ar** 39.948
4	potassium 19 **K** 39.098	calcium 20 **Ca** 40.078	scandium 21 **Sc** 44.956	titanium 22 **Ti** 47.867	vanadium 23 **V** 50.942	chromium 24 **Cr** 52.000	manganese 25 **Mn** 54.938	iron 26 **Fe** 55.845	cobalt 27 **Co** 58.933	nickel 28 **Ni** 58.693	copper 29 **Cu** 63.546	zinc 30 **Zn** 65.39	gallium 31 **Ga** 69.723	germanium 32 **Ge** 72.61	arsenic 33 **As** 74.922	selenium 34 **Se** 78.96	bromine 35 **Br** 79.904	krypton 36 **Kr** 83.80
5	rubidium 37 **Rb** 85.468	strontium 38 **Sr** 87.62	yttrium 39 **Y** 88.906	zirconium 40 **Zr** 91.22	niobium 41 **Nb** 92.910	molybdenum 42 **Mo** 95.94	technetium 43 **Tc** 97.91	ruthenium 44 **Ru** 101.07	rhodium 45 **Rh** 102.91	palladium 46 **Pd** 106.42	silver 47 **Ag** 107.87	cadmium 48 **Cd** 112.41	indium 49 **In** 114.82	tin 50 **Sn** 118.71	antimony 51 **Sb** 121.76	tellurium 52 **Te** 127.60	iodine 53 **I** 126.90	xenon 54 **Xe** 131.29
6	caesium 55 **Cs** 132.91	barium 56 **Ba** 137.33	57–71	hafnium 72 **Hf** 178.49	tantalum 73 **Ta** 180.95	tungsten 74 **W** 183.84	rhenium 75 **Re** 186.21	osmium 76 **Os** 190.23	iridium 77 **Ir** 192.22	platinum 78 **Pt** 195.08	gold 79 **Au** 196.97	mercury 80 **Hg** 200.59	thallium 81 **Tl** 204.38	lead 82 **Pb** 207.20	bismuth 83 **Bi** 208.98	polonium 84 **Po** [208.98]	astatine 85 **At** [209.99]	radon 86 **Rn** [222.02]
7	francium 87 **Fr** [223.02]	radium 88 **Ra** 226.03	89–103	rutherfordium 104 **Rf** [267.12]	dubnium 105 **Db** [268.13]	seaborgium 106 **Sg** [269.13]	bohrium 107 **Bh** [270.14]	hassium 108 **Hs** [269.15]	meitnerium 109 **Mt** [278.15]	darmstadtium 110 **Ds** [281.16]	roentgenium 111 **Rg** [281.17]	copernicium 112 **Cn** [285.17]	nihonium 113 **Nh** [286.18]	flerovium 114 **Fl** [289.18]	moscovium 115 **Mc** [289.19]	livermorium 116 **Lv** [293.15]	tennessine 117 **Ts** [294.13]	oganesson 118 **Og** [294.21]

Lanthanides

lanthanum 57 **La** 138.91	cerium 58 **Ce** 140.12	praseodymium 59 **Pr** 140.91	neodymium 60 **Nd** 144.24	promethium 61 **Pm** [144.92]	samarium 62 **Sm** 150.36	europium 63 **Eu** 151.96	gadolinium 64 **Gd** 157.25	terbium 65 **Tb** 158.93	dysprosium 66 **Dy** 162.50	holmium 67 **Ho** 164.93	erbium 68 **Er** 167.26	thulium 69 **Tm** 168.93	ytterbium 70 **Yb** 173.04	lutetium 71 **Lu** 174.97

Actinides

actinium 89 **Ac** [227.03]	thorium 90 **Th** 232.04	protactinium 91 **Pa** 231.04	uranium 92 **U** 238.03	neptunium 93 **Np** [237.05]	plutonium 94 **Pu** 244.06	americium 95 **Am** [243.06]	curium 96 **Cm** [247.07]	berkelium 97 **Bk** [247.07]	californium 98 **Cf** [251.08]	einsteinium 99 **Es** [252.08]	fermium 100 **Fm** [257.10]	mendelevium 101 **Md** [258.10]	nobelium 102 **No** [259.10]	lawrencium 103 **Lr** [262.12]

Relative atomic mass is the weighted mean of the atomic masses of all atoms of a chemical element found in a given sample, which is standardized in comparison to one-twelfth the mass of a carbon-12 atom. Replacing the term **atomic weight**, relative atomic mass is a more general term that may be applied to nonterrestrial and highly specific terrestrial environments. Therefore, two samples of an element that normally consists of more than one isotope, collected from two widely spaced natural sources on Earth, are expected to have relative atomic masses that differ very slightly.

The **atomic number** is unique to each chemical element. It denotes the number of protons found in the nucleus of an atom and is therefore identical to the charge number of the nucleus (also called valence). For an atom of neutral charge, the atomic number is equal to the number of electrons.

This copy of *Grids & Guides* has been updated to reflect the verification and renaming of four elements by the International Union of Pure and Applied Chemistry in 2016. Elements 113, 115, 117, and 118 now officially complete the 7th row, though many of their properties are still being studied.

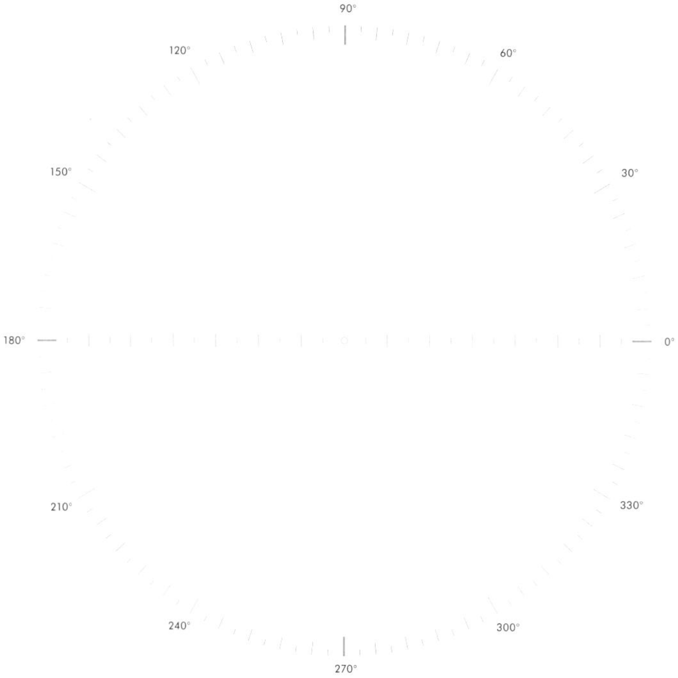

90°

120°   60°

150°   30°

180°   0°

210°   330°

240°   300°

270°

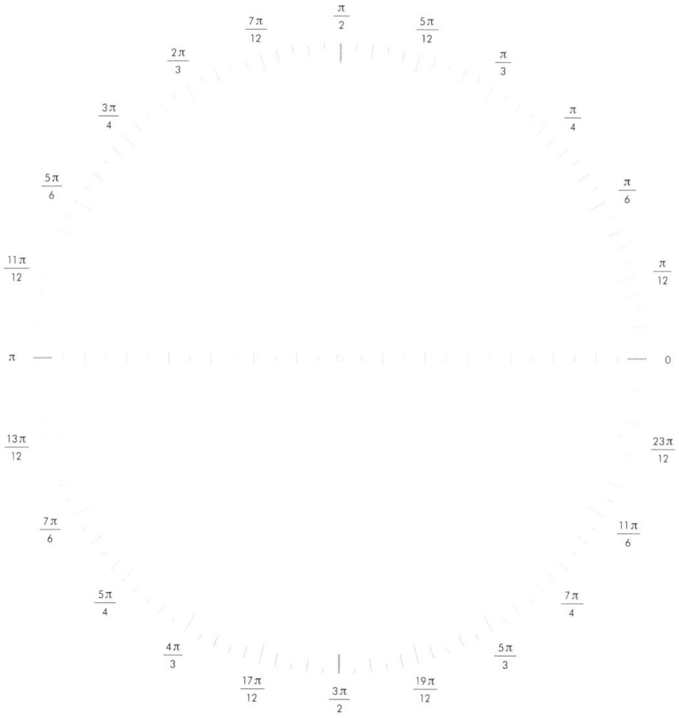

$\frac{7\pi}{12}$ $\frac{\pi}{2}$ $\frac{5\pi}{12}$

$\frac{2\pi}{3}$ $\frac{\pi}{3}$

$\frac{3\pi}{4}$ $\frac{\pi}{4}$

$\frac{5\pi}{6}$ $\frac{\pi}{6}$

$\frac{11\pi}{12}$ $\frac{\pi}{12}$

π 0

$\frac{13\pi}{12}$ $\frac{23\pi}{12}$

$\frac{7\pi}{6}$ $\frac{11\pi}{6}$

$\frac{5\pi}{4}$ $\frac{7\pi}{4}$

$\frac{4\pi}{3}$ $\frac{5\pi}{3}$

$\frac{17\pi}{12}$ $\frac{3\pi}{2}$ $\frac{19\pi}{12}$

1													
2													
3													
4													
5													
6													
7													
8													
9													
10													
11													
12													
13													
14													
15													
16													
17													
18													
19													
20													
21													
22													
23													
24													
25													
26													
27													
28													
29													
30													
31													
32													
33													
34													
35													
36													
37													
38													

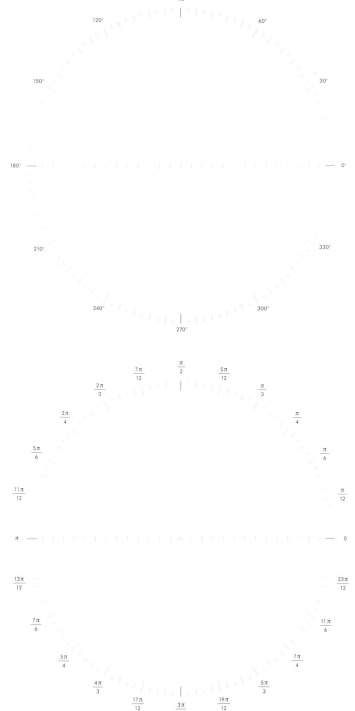

1														
2														
3														
4														
5														
6														
7														
8														
9														
10														
11														
12														
13														
14														
15														
16														
17														
18														
19														
20														
21														
22														
23														
24														
25														
26														
27														
28														
29														
30														
31														
32														
33														
34														
35														
36														
37														
38														

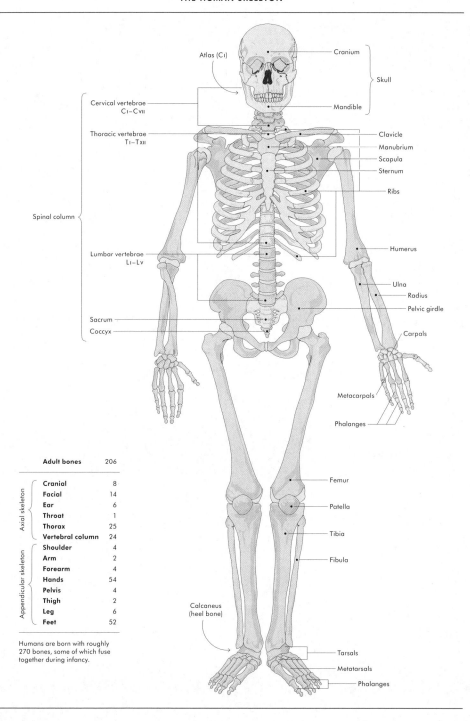

Atlas (C$_I$)

Cervical vertebrae
C$_I$–C$_{VII}$

Thoracic vertebrae
T$_I$–T$_{XII}$

Spinal column

Lumbar vertebrae
L$_I$–L$_V$

Sacrum
Coccyx

Cranium
Skull
Mandible
Clavicle
Manubrium
Scapula
Sternum
Ribs
Humerus
Ulna
Radius
Pelvic girdle
Carpals
Metacarpals
Phalanges
Femur
Patella
Tibia
Fibula
Calcaneus
(heel bone)
Tarsals
Metatarsals
Phalanges

Adult bones	206
Cranial	8
Facial	14
Ear	6
Throat	1
Thorax	25
Vertebral column	24
Shoulder	4
Arm	2
Forearm	4
Hands	54
Pelvis	4
Thigh	2
Leg	6
Feet	52

Axial skeleton

Appendicular skeleton

Humans are born with roughly
270 bones, some of which fuse
together during infancy.

Upper dial (degrees):

90°
120° 60°
150° 30°
180° —— 0°
210° 330°
240° 300°
270°

Lower dial (radians):

$\frac{\pi}{2}$
$\frac{7\pi}{12}$ $\frac{5\pi}{12}$
$\frac{2\pi}{3}$ $\frac{\pi}{3}$
$\frac{3\pi}{4}$ $\frac{\pi}{4}$
$\frac{5\pi}{6}$ $\frac{\pi}{6}$
$\frac{11\pi}{12}$ $\frac{\pi}{12}$
π —— 0
$\frac{13\pi}{12}$ $\frac{23\pi}{12}$
$\frac{7\pi}{6}$ $\frac{11\pi}{6}$
$\frac{5\pi}{4}$ $\frac{7\pi}{4}$
$\frac{4\pi}{3}$ $\frac{5\pi}{3}$
$\frac{17\pi}{12}$ $\frac{19\pi}{12}$
$\frac{3\pi}{2}$

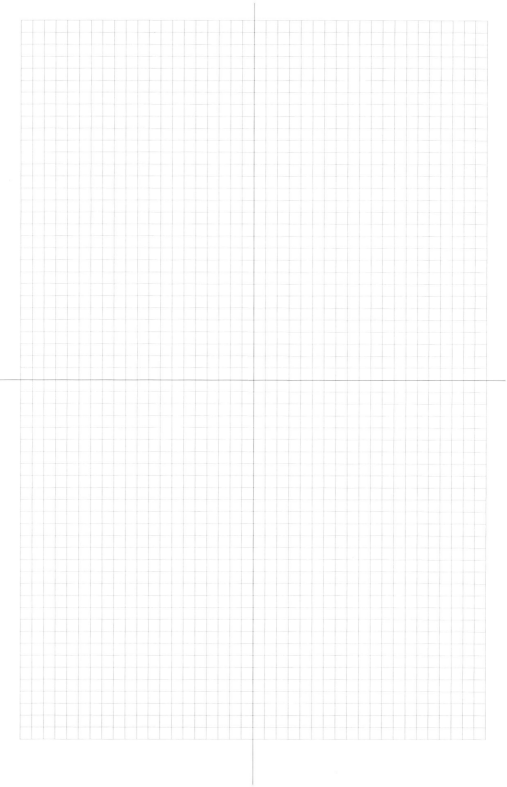

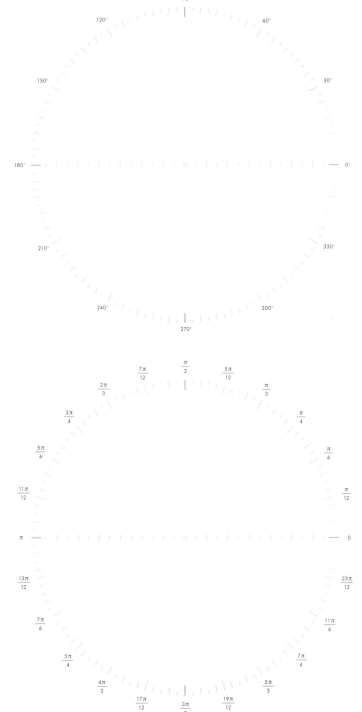

1												
2												
3												
4												
5												
6												
7												
8												
9												
10												
11												
12												
13												
14												
15												
16												
17												
18												
19												
20												
21												
22												
23												
24												
25												
26												
27												
28												
29												
30												
31												
32												
33												
34												
35												
36												
37												
38												

ORDERS OF MAGNITUDE

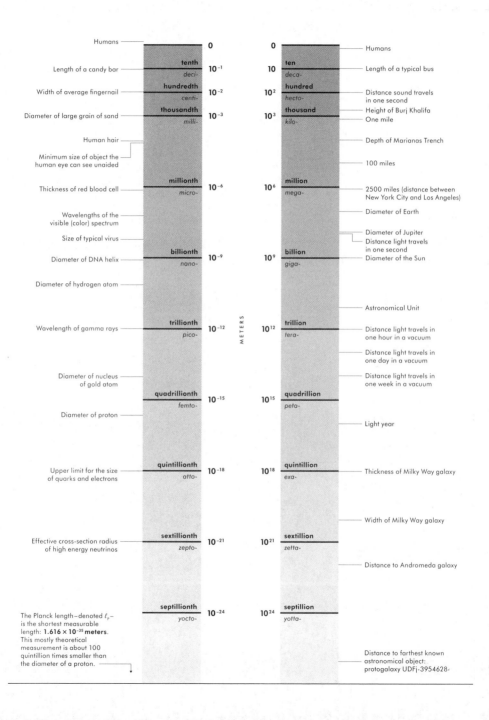

Humans — 0

Length of a candy bar — **tenth** / *deci-* — 10^{-1}

Width of average fingernail — **hundredth** / *centi-* — 10^{-2}

Diameter of large grain of sand — **thousandth** / *milli-* — 10^{-3}

Human hair —

Minimum size of object the human eye can see unaided —

Thickness of red blood cell — **millionth** / *micro-* — 10^{-6}

Wavelengths of the visible (color) spectrum —

Size of typical virus —

Diameter of DNA helix — **billionth** / *nano-* — 10^{-9}

Diameter of hydrogen atom —

Wavelength of gamma rays — **trillionth** / *pico-* — 10^{-12}

Diameter of nucleus of gold atom —

quadrillionth / *femto-* — 10^{-15}

Diameter of proton —

Upper limit for the size of quarks and electrons — **quintillionth** / *atto-* — 10^{-18}

sextillionth / *zepto-* — 10^{-21}
Effective cross-section radius of high energy neutrinos —

septillionth / *yocto-* — 10^{-24}

The Planck length—denoted ℓ_p— is the shortest measurable length: **1.616 × 10⁻³⁵ meters.** This mostly theoretical measurement is about 100 quintillion times smaller than the diameter of a proton. —

METERS

0
10 / *deca-* — Length of a typical bus
10^2 **hundred** / *hecto-* — Distance sound travels in one second
10^3 **thousand** / *kilo-* — Height of Burj Khalifa / One mile

— Depth of Marianas Trench

— 100 miles

10^6 **million** / *mega-* — 2500 miles (distance between New York City and Los Angeles)
— Diameter of Earth

— Diameter of Jupiter
— Distance light travels in one second
10^9 **billion** / *giga-* — Diameter of the Sun

— Astronomical Unit

10^{12} **trillion** / *tera-* — Distance light travels in one hour in a vacuum
— Distance light travels in one day in a vacuum
— Distance light travels in one week in a vacuum

10^{15} **quadrillion** / *peta-*
— Light year

10^{18} **quintillion** / *exa-* — Thickness of Milky Way galaxy

— Width of Milky Way galaxy

10^{21} **sextillion** / *zetta-*
— Distance to Andromeda galaxy

10^{24} **septillion** / *yotta-*

— Distance to farthest known astronomical object: protogalaxy UDFj-3954628

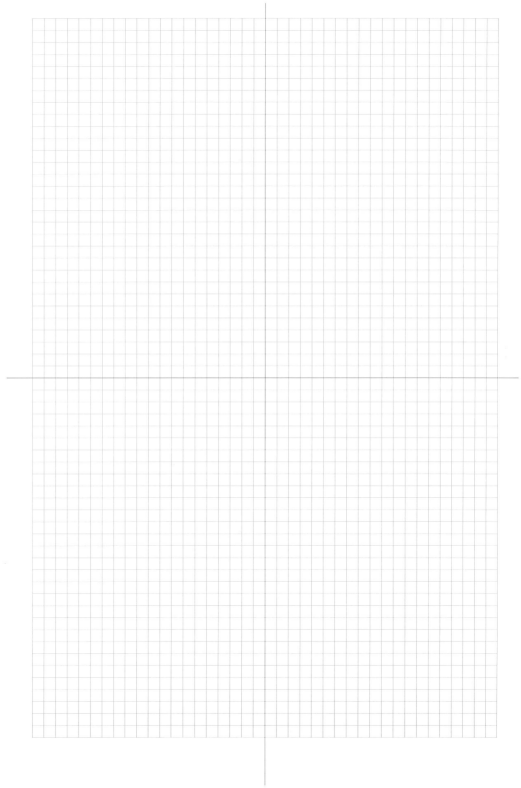

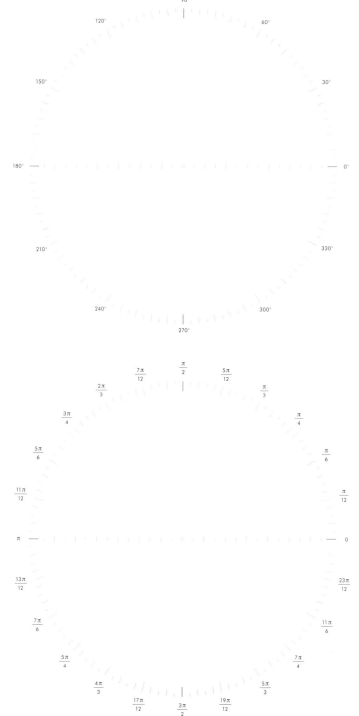

1												
2												
3												
4												
5												
6												
7												
8												
9												
10												
11												
12												
13												
14												
15												
16												
17												
18												
19												
20												
21												
22												
23												
24												
25												
26												
27												
28												
29												
30												
31												
32												
33												
34												
35												
36												
37												
38												

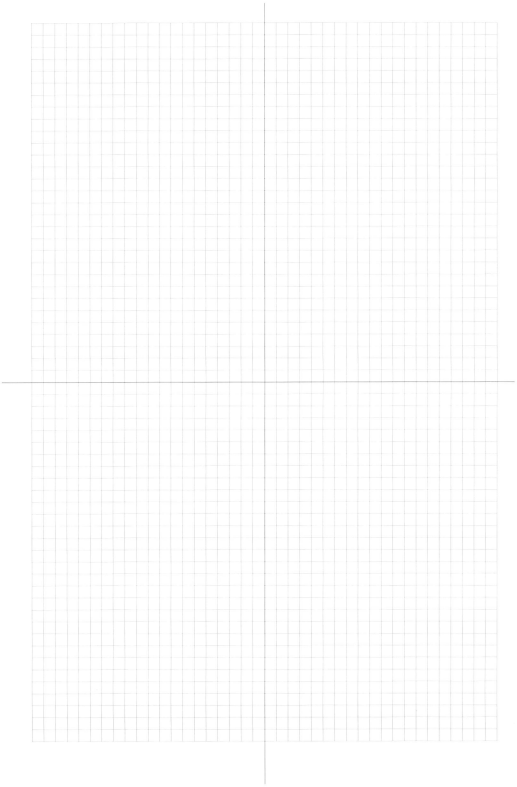

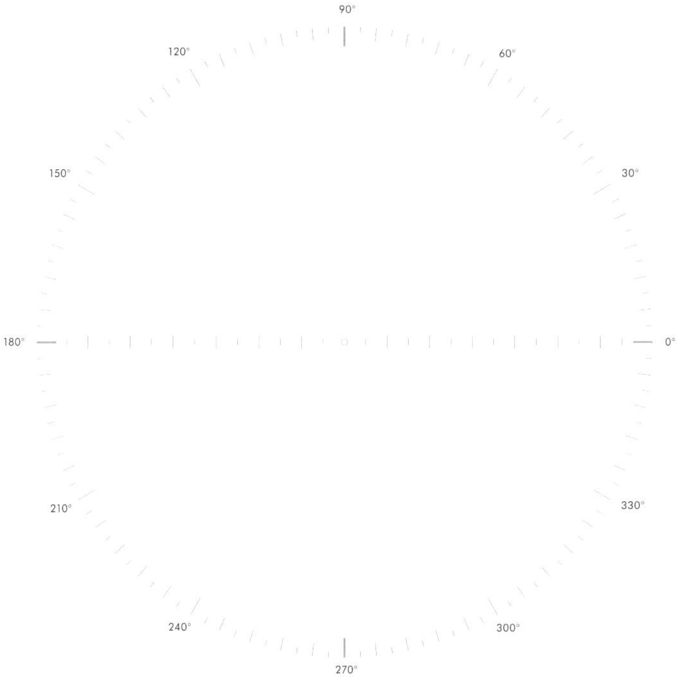

Two circular protractor/angle dials. Upper dial labeled in degrees:

90°
120° 60°
150° 30°
180° 0°
210° 330°
240° 300°
270°

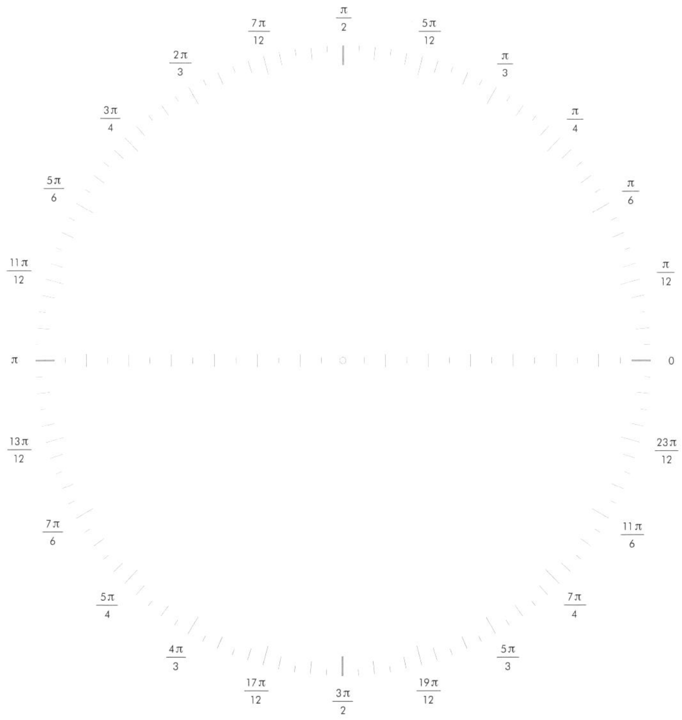

Lower dial labeled in radians:

$\frac{\pi}{2}$
$\frac{7\pi}{12}$ $\frac{5\pi}{12}$
$\frac{2\pi}{3}$ $\frac{\pi}{3}$
$\frac{3\pi}{4}$ $\frac{\pi}{4}$
$\frac{5\pi}{6}$ $\frac{\pi}{6}$
$\frac{11\pi}{12}$ $\frac{\pi}{12}$
π 0
$\frac{13\pi}{12}$ $\frac{23\pi}{12}$
$\frac{7\pi}{6}$ $\frac{11\pi}{6}$
$\frac{5\pi}{4}$ $\frac{7\pi}{4}$
$\frac{4\pi}{3}$ $\frac{5\pi}{3}$
$\frac{17\pi}{12}$ $\frac{3\pi}{2}$ $\frac{19\pi}{12}$

1											
2											
3											
4											
5											
6											
7											
8											
9											
10											
11											
12											
13											
14											
15											
16											
17											
18											
19											
20											
21											
22											
23											
24											
25											
26											
27											
28											
29											
30											
31											
32											
33											
34											
35											
36											
37											
38											

SIMPLE HARMONIC MOTION
Pendulum

In the small-angle approximation, the motion of a simple pendulum is approximated by simple harmonic motion. The period of a mass attached to a pendulum of length **L** and gravitational acceleration **g** is given by the equation:

$$T = 2\pi \sqrt{\frac{L}{g}}$$

The period of oscillation is independent of the amplitude and mass of the pendulum but not gravitational acceleration. This approximation is accurate only in small angles because the expression for angular acceleration is proportional to the sine of position:

$$mgL \sin(\theta) = I\alpha$$

where **I** is the moment of inertia. When θ is small, $\sin \theta \approx \theta$ and therefore the expression becomes:

$$-mgL\theta = I\alpha$$

which makes angular acceleration directly proportional to θ, satisfying the definition of simple harmonic motion.

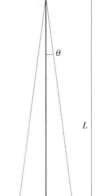

SIMPLE HARMONIC MOTION
Spring

A mass attached to a spring exhibits simple harmonic motion in closed space. The period of a mass **m** attached to a spring with spring constant **k** is given by the equation:

$$T = 2\pi \sqrt{\frac{m}{k}}$$

The period of oscillation is independent of both the amplitude and gravitational acceleration. Hooke's Law states that the force **F** required to extend or compress a spring by a certain distance, Δ**x**, is proportional to that distance, given by the equation:

$$F = k\Delta x$$

The spring constant **k** is a measure of the spring's stiffness and depends on its material and construction.

KINEMATICS
Projectile Motion

$$v = \frac{\Delta x}{\Delta t}$$

$$v = v_\circ + at$$

$$x = x_\circ + v_\circ t + \frac{1}{2} at^2$$

$$a = g = 9.8 \text{ m/s}^2$$

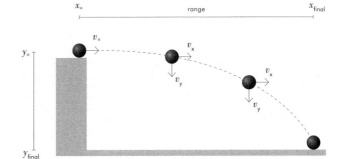

Newton's Laws of Motion

FIRST LAW
An object at rest remains at rest unless acted upon by a force. An object in motion remains in motion, and at a constant velocity, unless acted upon by a force.

$$\frac{F}{m} = \frac{F}{m}$$

SECOND LAW
The acceleration of a body is directly proportional to, and in the same direction as, the net force acting on the body, and inversely proportional to its mass. Thus, **F = ma**, where **F** is the net force acting on the object, **m** is the mass of the object, and **a** is the acceleration of the object.

THIRD LAW
When one body exerts a force on a second body, the second body simultaneously exerts a force equal in magnitude and opposite in direction to that of the first body.

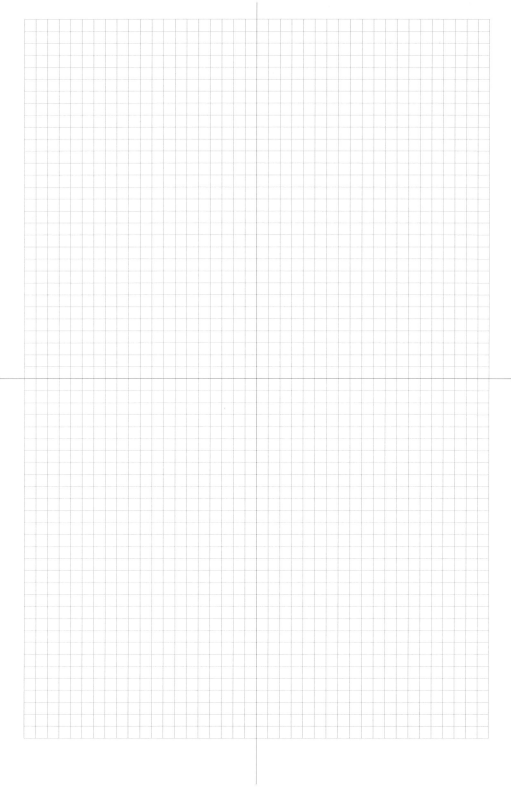

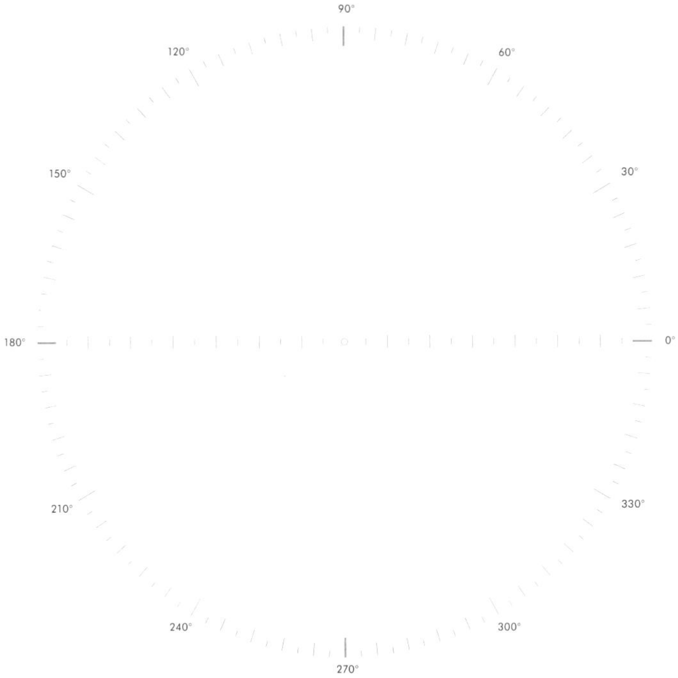
90°
60°
30°
0°
330°
300°
270°
240°
210°
180°
150°
120°

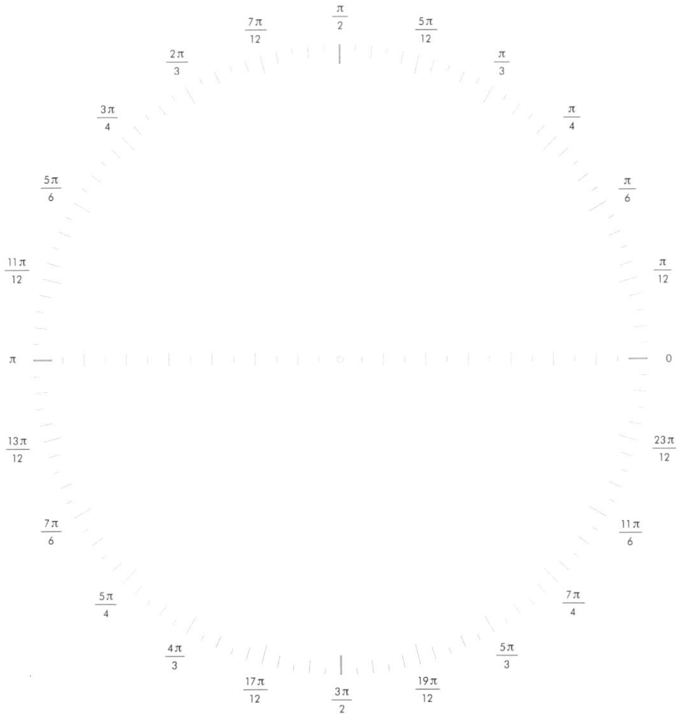
π/2
5π/12
π/3
π/4
π/6
π/12
0
23π/12
11π/6
7π/4
5π/3
19π/12
3π/2
17π/12
4π/3
5π/4
7π/6
13π/12
π
11π/12
5π/6
3π/4
2π/3
7π/12

1										
2										
3										
4										
5										
6										
7										
8										
9										
10										
11										
12										
13										
14										
15										
16										
17										
18										
19										
20										
21										
22										
23										
24										
25										
26										
27										
28										
29										
30										
31										
32										
33										
34										
35										
36										
37										
38										

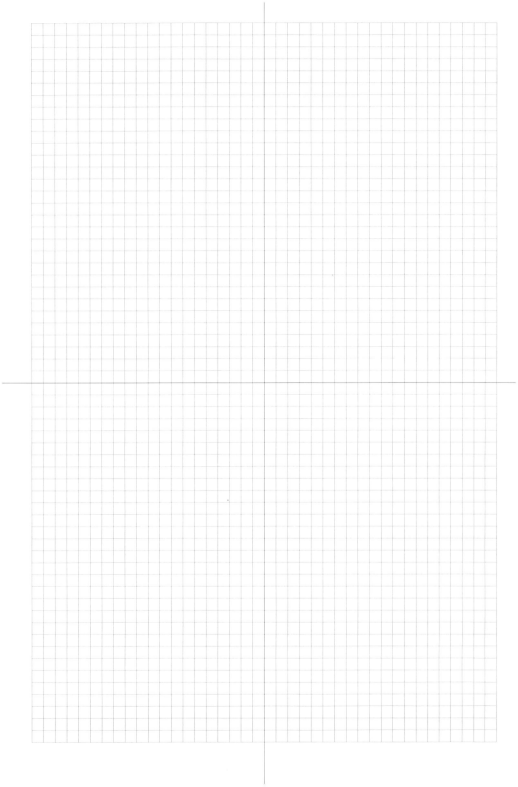